Whispers from the Heart

Antoinette Jewett

BALBOA.
PRESS
A DIVISION OF HAY HOUSE

Balboa Press books may be ordered through booksellers or by contacting:

Balboa Press
A Division of Hay House
1663 Liberty Drive
Bloomington, IN 47403
www.balboapress.com
1 (877) 407-4847

Because of the dynamic nature of the Internet, any web addresses or
links contained in this book may have changed since publication and may
no longer be valid. The views expressed in this work are solely those
of the author and do not necessarily reflect the views of the publisher,
and the publisher hereby disclaims any responsibility for them.

The author of this book does not dispense medical advice or prescribe
the use of any technique as a form of treatment for physical, emotional,
or medical problems without the advice of a physician, either directly or
indirectly. The intent of the author is only to offer information of a general
nature and for your reading enjoyment. In the event you use any of the
information in this book for yourself, which is your constitutional right,
the author and the publisher assume no responsibility for your actions.

Any people depicted in stock imagery provided by Getty Images are
models, and such images are being used for illustrative purposes only.
Certain stock imagery © Getty Images.

Print information available on the last page.

ISBN: 978-1-5043-9840-4 (sc)
ISBN: 978-1-5043-9841-1 (e)

Library of Congress Control Number: 2018902103

Balboa Press rev. date: 11/19/2018

Contents

Sing Your Own Song

A small brown bird came to church today.

It flew into the rafters and stayed quite hidden.

But when the organ began to play and its notes rose

High into the air. The bird flapped its wings and

Sang its heart out, uncalled for, nor unbidden.

If its voice was good, was without thought or wit,

It just sang its own praises to Heaven.

"Alone, I sit in my sacred space,
My mind open to trailing ribbons of thought.
Some are knotted, some tangled.
But whispers emerge ever clear and true,
Unbound and freely offered."

♡

The whispers came...
I listened...
Then, I wrote the words...

Dedication Page

I dedicate this book to my cherished family,
who are my greatest blessings and
my source of happiness.
I dearly love you all.
Thank you for your never ending love and support.
You are all my dreams come true.

I also dedicate this book to my
dearest, lifelong friends.
It is love that binds us together,
Our friendships are a treasure.

I am grateful for a full heart.
♡ ♡ ♡ ♡

"I sit alone in a sacred place,
alone in the presence of nature."

♡

Before The Dawn

Come sit with me in the stillness of the morning.
Listen to the gentle whispers of the swaying trees,
The laughter of flowers as they dance across meadows,
To the symphony of life breaking the silence.
Ponder the universe, tinted in
Colors from a rainbow sky.
Harken to heaven's yearnings
And those of your heart.
Arms open wide, embrace each
Morning's pristine light,
Inhale the hushed, fresh breath
Of a new morn's majesty.
Come sit with me before the dawn.

*"Take time to ponder the moments,
seek more than the eyes can see."*

♡

A Tattered Rose

A tattered rose
Clinging on slender stem,
Cast forth a fragrance sweet.
On the breath of a breeze,
It was carried to me.
My senses filled,
I saw naught,
Its weathered edges.

"Not every gift given,
comes with
paper and ribbon."

A Gift

Petals hushed,
By an evening's breath,
Float, cast on a comely breeze.
A rose's portion of itself,
Surrendered to waiting hands
And gathered on bended knees.

"A promise born is yours to find."

A Promise Born

Deeply within a promise born,
Measured out on heaven's new morn,
When seeds of greatness came your way,
Tenderly planted there to stay.
Your precious gift you cannot scorn.

What greatness do you have inborn,
You tremble feeling so forlorn,
A possibility achieved,
Too far beyond to be conceived.
A cloak of honor you adorn.

Do not wander or go astray,
Let courage be your strength each day,
Believe in all that's good and kind,
A promise born is yours to find.
Follow your heart, it leads the way.

"Someone to lean on,

someone to love."

♡

I Was Only Two And You Were Brand New

Our journey began a long time ago,
I was only two and you were brand new.
The moment I saw you, what could I do
But love you forever. My face all aglow.
My precious doll with hair painted, just so.
With red lips to kiss and cheeks with a blush,
Eyebrows designed with the swipe of a brush.
Your tongue and teeth were unusual to see,
Made you all that much more special to me.

"Faith comforts a saddened heart."

♡

But everything changed when I turned just four
And you my baby had aged by two years.
Our lives would be different than before.
My big happy smiles turned into sad tears.
By myself, I would fly so far away,
Off to fair England and there I would stay.
I hugged you tight, I did not understand,
Leaving my parents, for an unknown land
And leave you all alone, how could that be,
We would go together, baby and me.

"We are never alone."

♡

Side by side we cuddled, in the dark plane,

Peering into shadows and pouring rain.

Our journey long, a quiet mystery,

Enveloped in mists of sadness, I see.

My aching heart needed comfort and love,

You, baby were strong and leaned against me.

I saw Jesus and His angels above.

Life has its way, with its twists and its turns,

For when you are small and not very tall,

You lean on faith and a big, baby doll.

I was only two and you were brand new.

"Nature has her way
of pulling on heart strings."

♡

Rocked By The Wind

Rocked by the wind,
They ride on a breeze,
A mother bird's eggs,
Swaying with ease.
So neatly tucked in,
With fluff
And with down.

Five blue eggs,
With ten baby legs,
Are rocked by the wind,
As they ride on a breeze,
A planter their cradle,
Their mother a mantle.

Space is tight,
But feels just right.
When rocked by the wind
And riding a breeze.

"Wishing you blue flower mornings,
With roses entwined.
Sunbeams and butterflies,
Blessed by the Divine."

A Gathering Of Blue

Glass beads of true blue, roll
across the floor and pass
on through the azure door, gathering
sunlight in their play,
spreading blue rays to brighten my way.

A path of posies cobalt blue, with
fragrance sweet, caress
my feet on this very special, cool blue day.
The careless wind tugs on ribbons,
sky blue, tied to a ponytail

"A single blue flower,
A simple love note,
Forget-me-not."

pulling them through to places far,
adventures unknown, gone to
where lost ribbons must go.

Eyes look my way with pensive
thought and do what eyes must
do, they blink their lashes up at me
and I surrender to a sea of blue.
Enclosed in shells of robin blue, a
bird's speckled eggs promise
life anew.
All tucked in a nest with beads
of blue, cobalt posies lay
there too, with wind tossed
ribbons woven through…

I see amongst a gathering of blue.

"Why suffer over broken pieces, when with time you may have someone whole."

The China Vase

The china vase lay broken, scattered
upon the unyielding floor.
Each gently, painted petal separated
from its appointed place.
No longer recognized, a puzzle
of despair before my eyes.
The vase a gift of beauty, that had been
fondled and treasured, now had sharp edges,
it's purpose and value forever lost.
Once it was filled with life, nurturing
the glory so freely offered to a meaningful
existence, filled with hope and love.

"Blessings arise from the fragments of despair."

♡

Each shattered piece looked upon, as it
reflected memories of a lifetime. A marriage
that once held the promise of eternity.
Children's laughter quickly
silenced, dreams fragmented,
carelessly forgotten and tossed to a wailing wind.
Hopes crushed into the useless
fragments, as small as those
of the china vase, smashed without forethought.

Slowly the pieces are gathered, some
still too painful to hold.
Others carry memories that will
always remain in the heart.

"Broken dreams,

Broken promises,

Broken ties,

Broken hearts,

May all be mended,

When you love another."

The vase is forever broken, but a
deep and abiding faith makes
a broken heart, forever whole.

A smiling face, a warm embrace,
I am offered a new china vase.

"When we open our eyes to beauty,
we see it everywhere."

♡

A New Morn

I see roses blooming, red ones,
Swaying, now cloaked in morning dew,
Glittering gems tossed far and wide.
Apples prancing on weighted boughs.

Joyful twitters filling hushed air,
Enameled sun on land and sea.
Meadows revel in freshness found,
Pristine daisies dance the hillsides.

Resting herds stirring, skies blueing,
Murmurings punctuate silence.
Blinking eyes open, gladness born,
Herald the dawn of this new morn.

*"Divine guidance shows us the way,
but we are the ones who choose the path."*

♡

Heaven's Earth

Sweet flowers bend to kiss the earth,
Swift gusts of wind express their mirth,
Sweeping across wide empty plains,
To rise and fall with earth's terrains.
Soil murmurs secrets long untold,
Listen with care they will unfold.
Deep canyons hold our memories,
Of lifelong tender reveries.

The warm earth enshrouds our sorrows,
Holding on for bright tomorrows.
Seedlings of hope emerge each year
And faith replaces all our fear.

"Embrace the hills and the valleys of life,
wherever you may wander."

♡

Whispers escape a vital breeze,
Sink to the earth on bended knees.
With hands pressed to an open sky,
Hear now the lost soul's wailful cry.

Lie prone upon life's dusty ridge,
Connect ourselves to heaven's bridge.
Lifting us up to greater heights,
Now unfettered for higher flights.
Keen eyes wander the cloudless skies,
Stains purged, kept promises arise.
Climbing renewed, joyful rebirth,
We shepherd paths of heaven's earth.

"Love eternal, love divine,
life's greatest gift,
that you are mine."

Sew Me, So That...

Sew me into your coat,
So that I may feel your warmth.
Sew me into the seams of your heart,
So that I will feel your tenderness.
Sew me with the threads of your thoughts,
So that our minds may understand.
Sew me with your fingers laced with mine,
So that we will walk hand in hand.
Sew me with the bonds of your love,
So that we may stand on hallowed ground.
Together.

"When we become quiet,
that's when the enchantment begins."

Listen

I hear music
from an eternal place,
Tugging, pulling
on the yearnings
of my heart.
Dancing in the depths
of my soul...
Rippling,
Embracing,
Rising, falling,
Swirling notes,

"Music wraps itself around the soul."

♡

Soothing,
Peaceful,
Healing.

Wrapped in this cocoon of bliss,
Embraced in pure delight,
My body sings in unison,
With its pulsating melody.
Sublime music,
Coming from a higher place,
That we may still remember.

"When one heart gives,

two receive."

A Time So Long Ago

The music box holds memories of a
time so long ago, now forgotten
and covered with dust, it idly rests, no
notes escape its beautiful case.
Oh, I remember the times when it was
played, over and over again.
Beautiful music with tinkling notes,
drawing thoughts back to
"Remember when."
Those days of old when love was
young and hopes were as high
as a summer sky.

"Love embraces two hearts and makes them one."

♡

Our love was sweet with joy divine,
when promises were made
and you were mine.
The music played as life passed us
by, as we listened to laughter
and our baby's first cry. Singing
songs and dancing along to the
music of long ago.
As the lid of the box is now lifted,
one final note escapes.
My mind reflects upon joyful moments,
another time, another place.
So much I had forgotten, until
I heard that note so pure
drawing forth treasured memories of you, my love,
in a time so long ago.

*"Mother Nature is very wise
and generous with her lessons."*

♡

The Daylily

Each morning, a stunning Daylily
flower blooms for only one day.
All that it has to give is offered
for those few precious hours.
The blossom shows its vibrant
beauty, its sensitive markings,
the incredible fire burning deeply
within its tender heart.
No other bloom will ever be exactly the same.

Its beauty is abundant and intense,
or at times a gentle
splash of color riding high on a spirited breeze.

"Beauty comes straight from the heart."

♡

Another flower replaces the first spent blossom,
Its radiance also glows and lasts for just a day.

Daily, there are moments for us
to offer our very best.
It may be for only one given moment,
a few hours, or a lifetime,
for us to share what an incredible gift we each are,
to this beautiful world.

"Seek the beauty you have never seen,
embrace the wonders you have never sought."

♡

Embrace

Be generous with yourself. A library is not
complete with one book sitting on empty shelves.
Open the pages of your mind,
your spirit, your being,
Surround yourself with wisdom
and ripples of laughter.
Peer down a rabbit hole, inhale earth's memories,
Hitch a ride on a stunning butterfly's wings,
Soar high on the breath of an eternal dream.

Catch fibers of tomorrow and weave them today,
Part veils of mist, smell new
thoughts of the future.

"Wander the depths of your longings"

♡

Caress the fabric of the air, chase the cobwebs
Of the winds and finger the sheerness of petals.
Drink in points of light from a chalice of stardust,
Rise with the sun's brilliance permeating your soul
And nightly, be cradled in
moonbeams and starlight.

"Precious beyond understanding."

A Miracle

Today I hold a miracle,
Wrapped in my warm embrace.
I gaze into her precious eyes,
Her sweet adoring face.
Today I hold a miracle,
From God's own hands to mine.

No words express my gratitude,
So gracious, so divine.
Today I hold a miracle,
A gift so dearly given.
A darling little baby girl,
Stella, a star, straight from heaven.

"A star is shining and its light leads the way."

♡

Heaven's Star

Heaven's star twinkling brightly,
A mystery in action catches my earnest gaze.
What message is there to be found, that holds
My presence in this given sacred moment.
Perhaps your purpose was fulfilled,
Oh, so long ago
When a precious babe bathed in your holy light.
Now your glowing reflects a path, a knowing, for
My life to follow as I wander on this earth.
Stunning star, what is your purpose now,
Casting glory in your own special place.
Are you teaching me to shine, to radiate as you,
The gracious glory of the Divine.

*"We are all connected,
by an eternal thread of light."*

♡

I see you hanging there on your cosmic string,
Your brilliance takes my breath away.
So far and yet you touch my humble life,
My thoughts, my awe, my breathless gratitude.

Heaven's star you remind me of my Savior's love,
each time I see you shining.

*"Seek to lift another
and you shall find yourself uplifted."*

♡

Baby Robin

Soft grey feathers, speckled breast,
A baby robin comes to rest.
New morning's light reflects the day,
As little robin comes to play.
Still too young, it cannot fly,
But flops and flutters to get by.
Souls need an uplifting word,
Prayers are lifted to be heard,
Heaven's breath,
Lifts the wing of a bird.

"It is the difficult times that encourage our greatest strengths."

♡

Hang On

Eerie darkness enveloped the fading
sun's last withering beam.
The hair raising wind's woeful
anthem, wild and free blew
down thorn, choked pathways, it's
whistling, screeching wails bounced
off of the dark threatening clouds of heaven.

The deafening roar reached its height
on a wayward hill, crested by
a crumbling mansion. Windows
splintered, glittering shards of glass
carelessly flung on a restless breath.

*"Hope emerges as a feather
and rises on the wings of an eagle."*

♡

The tattoo of slapping shutters fractured
the silence, hanging as a pall over
this spine, chilling eventide.

A massive riveted door rumbled and
groaned, as it was ripped
from its rusted hinges by the determined
clutches of a massive force.
No competition for the strength of nature, it was
hurled into dust particles of yesterday's memories.
Biting nails viciously flung, to inflict
pain on any lost soul who dared to
venture out to face the wind's fury.
Heads tucked under wings and
creatures in their burrows,
await the passing of the tempest.

"Never give up."

At the height of the bluster a sudden calm,
as gentle as a prayer, permeated the air.
Modest twitters wafted from the twisted
rafters, as rays of forbidden light fingered
their way through rain-split clouds.

Warmth, where there had been chill.
Peace, when all was thought lost.
Hope, where there had been none.
Yet, in the deafening silence,
Children's laughter drifted to the heavens,
As a small, green leaf, clinging
to a splintered bough,
danced on a softened breeze.

"Time heals,
impatience hurts."

♡

Patience

I hold a tender flower bud,
With frailty, trembling on the bush.
Its petals now firmly folded,
Each dusted with a subtle blush.

I visualize them open wide,
Now bathing in new morning's ray.
But lingering, they calmly wait,
Securely wrapped, they gently lay.

"Patience offers its own reward."

♡

I wish the petals I could bend,
From the damp, new blossom's retreat.
Pull ruffled edges to unfurl,
Deeply inhale its fragrance sweet.

I hesitate, my hand withdraws,
All hope and promise will be lost.
My rash desires, too early met,
Destroy the dream, at what sad cost.

"It's the fragrance that holds the memories."

♡

The Fragrance

Perfume sweet, permeates the air, stirring
the fond remembrance of a friendship, both a gift,
my friend and the ever present stargazer lily.
The fragrance of both intermingled.

Each truly radiant, reflecting love of life,
exuding serene well being and the joy of living.
Memories neatly bound with ties to my heart,
pull upon the treasures of a lifetime.

Stargazers splattered pink, with carefree circles,
simple needs appointed for flower and friend, to

"If I breathe deeply enough, I still remember."

♡

spread their dazzling splendor and profound scent.
Life is inhaled, vital for both.

Passing time diminishes, loved ones and lilies
lose their strength, the beauty of both grows dim.
But deeply within, the fragrance
and rich splendor of the soul

remain constant.

Breathing becomes difficult, vitality lacking.
The fading plant rests undisturbed upon the dresser.
Its sweet fragrance, as one last embrace,
envelopes my frail sweet friend.
The perfume of both become one.

The fragrance lasts long after the flower is spent.

"Be still, the whispers will come ."

♡

The Whispers

I listened and joy spilt forth upon me like
a warm, comforting blanket of love.
I am not alone, wherever I wander.
I do not have all the answers, but daily
the quiet whispers can guide my footsteps.
If only, I will listen to that still, small voice
and walk the gentler path.

"Fear climbs upon a dark horse and takes you on a frantic ride."

♡

Love's A Wild Horse

Still again, I see him stand on yonder hill,

His snorting breath, misty vapors

in the morning air.

For the sweetness of the past he yearns,

Those tender moments shared by two and yet,

His nature wild and free, ever

pulls a wandering heart.

Tossing one, long yearning glance upon me,

He feels the bittersweet, what might have been.

Forgotten moments, ever rising as the sun,

Warm and fill a pounding heart.

"It is difficult to hold on to a wayward wind."

♡

A pause, eyes meet and glisten in the early rays,
Still again, he shakes his head in wild abandon,
Dismissing all that hinders a driven mind.
One last echoing whiney escapes on anxious breath,
Across the parched, endless
plains of life he gallops,
With wind so cruel, tearing at his heaving chest,
Where a forgotten heart of love, still ever beats.
He must forge forward, 'tis happiness he seeks.
Still again, I see him stand on yonder hill…

*"The simplest of pleasures give us
the most unexpected delight."*

♡

The Plucked Apricot

The first plucked apricot from my laden tree,
was full in my hand.
Fragrant, delicious, it's sweetened juice delicate
and satisfying.
Filling my yearning mouth with the warmth
of sunbeams.

"Sharing life's sweet moments together,
is what we tend to treasure."

Guilty Pleasures

You always eat the chocolates I favor,
You always guzzle my soft drink's last drop.
The pizza's thick crust goes down with a grunt.
Oh! I cannot believe you ate the lot.

Gooey frosting stuck to your sticky lips,
Tells the story that the cake is now gone.
Great Grandma's cookies are a plate of crumbs,
So you did not let them last, very long.

In a cloud of powdered sugar inhaled,
The wedding cookies just could not be saved.

"Sharing is caring."

♡

Then, fudge balls are stuffed in your eager mouth,
It's the sugar that makes you ill behaved.

I have watched you devour each tasty treat,
With that sweet smirk on your face, so sublime.
I smother a sly smile, while all the while
Wishing, those guilty pleasures had been mine.

"Do our wings lift us high enough."

♡

Wings

Deep within my heart a butterfly's wings unfurl,
Too long has it lain warm and secure.
Now it must come forth and spread
Its wings of glory.

Hark, airy wings all a flutter,
Not a word do I dare utter.
The air is still,
As my gaze falls upon
A mythical delight.
Gossamer wings,
Ethereal fairy in flight.

"*Dreams may be lost,
but never forgotten.*"

A Crown

A crown was placed upon my head,
With all the pomp and glory,
Its glittering jewels and polished gold,
Certainly promised a fairy tale story.

Not all fairy tales end with crowns,
Sometimes, coaches turn into pumpkins.
We lose our way and our silver slippers
And find ourselves in a pile of ashes.

But crowns can be worn by anyone, who is
True and brave of heart.

"Create your own fairy tale."

Seek a crown of unconditional love,
A crown of honesty.
A crown of forgiveness, for yourself
And for those who have offended.
This story has not ended.
A crown of service to others,
A crown of patience,
A crown of gratitude
And finally,
A crown of humility,
That you carry in your heart, with all
Of the other crowns you have sought.

That's when your fairy tale begins…

"When you shut the door to giving,
you have closed the portals to receiving."

Turn The Key

Take this key to unlock your heart,
Do not be afraid, just start.
What will you find. Why the tears.
The dreams, the wishes,
The hopes and the fears,
Have been locked up tightly,
Inside of you for years.
Now is the time for turning the key.
With shaking hands, you set yourself free,

"With arms open wide
embrace this beautiful world."

♡

To adventures unknown, just wait and see,

What possibilities are waiting,

When you turn the key.

Belief, Acceptance, Self-Love and Action.

"Deeply within,
unfulfilled dreams,

tug at the seams

of your heart."

A Time

There is a timing in all things.
A time for action,
A time to love,
A time for creativity,
A time to make a difference.
A time to leap,
A time to do something wonderful,
That you have never done before.

*"Memories are life's precious moments,
securely wrapped and tied with a love knot"*

Sweet Memories

Come walk with me down the Donkey
Lane, covered with blackberries,
beware they stain. See the bluebells
that brighten our way,
with heads bent in humility. They cover
deep woods in lavender blue,
as far as the eye can see. A heavenly scent drifts
through the air, telling where shy violets play.

Chase golden hills of primroses
and rest upon beds of glory.
Embrace scented petals, harken to a calling
bird's cry, all the while gazing

*"Oh, how delight lingers in
the spaces, between the beats of my heart."*

♡

to a grey, English sky.
Listen, you will hear the sigh
of a babbling stream,
where we can wade and cool our feet,
the rustle of rabbits hiding in
bushes or the scurry of mice
as we pass by.

With your lunch in a hankie,
tiptoe with me through thick,
green grass and you will see where the fairies hide,
in a beautiful, mossy fairy ring, where they
dance unseen and we can take time for afternoon
tea, with dainty, cream cakes to nibble on.
Later, we'll fashion daisy chains and
I shall crown you Fairy Queen of the
prettiest meadows, ever to be seen.

"Inhale the drift of the wildflowers."

♡

Feel the waning sun upon your face, the
silence of this hallowed place,
where Mother Nature has given her best,
all beautifully designed in holiness.
She drapes the sky with mist filled clouds and
fills the air with the sweet perfume of a thousand
flowers, softly bathed in morning showers.

The rich, damp earth absorbs the
moisture and there is a stillness in
the air, a sacredness that makes one
feel there are no others, just
you and I, who stand in this secret
place where beauty resides.
The silence holds only the whispers
of a gentle breeze filled with

*"Minds may wander, but they always seem
to walk us back to our childhood."*

♡

cherished memories of a lifetime,
playing where delight abides.

Told to be home before the bats fly, two
gleeful young girls, with berry stained faces
and three quarter tears in their carefree
smocked dresses, meander home from their jolly
day, gathering bluebells along their way.
Tender, sweet memories tucked into
young hearts, treasured and
there to stay.
Oh, to walk down that path again
and breathe in the freshness of
a cool English rain.

There are only so many letters
in the alphabet, but when
combined in a variety of ways,
to form words, they create magic.
Enticingly, beautiful magic.

Shout and the words may echo
throughout the world.
A whisper can shake a universe.

May we strive
to remember our beginnings,
for we all come from one source.
We have connections,
there is no end…

About The Author

Antoinette Jewett's love of writing began in a small village, in southern England, where she was born.

Later, she felt the pull to capture the feelings and whispers that have been tugging long, on her yearning heart.

She dearly loves spending time with her children and family. In her spare time, she enjoys painting with watercolors, pen and ink and creating detailed, colored pencil drawings.